NATIONAL GEOGRAPHIC

STAR POWER

PIONEER EDITION

By Don Thomas and Elizabeth Sengel

CONTENTS

OUR STAR, THE SUN

By Don Thomas

NASA ASTRONAUT

Follow an astronaut on his journey to the stars.

I had been waiting for this moment since I was six years old.

I was strapped in my seat on the space shuttle *Columbia*. It was minutes before takeoff. Suddenly, the rocket engines roared to life.

We lifted off. *Columbia* shot upward. "Yahoo!" I yelled. "Let's go!" My first trip into space had begun.

Minutes later, everything went silent. The main engines cut off. Another wave of excitement hit me. I realized we'd made it. I was in space. What would I see there?

Sunrise, Sunset

I unstrapped my seat belt and floated to a window. The view took my breath away. Space was darker than any other color I had ever seen. In the distance, a thin blue crescent glowed. It was Earth's atmosphere.

Soon, I saw my first sunset in space. As Earth spins on its **axis**, it makes one **rotation** every 24 hours. On Earth, we see one sunrise and one sunset each day. *Columbia* orbited Earth once every 90 minutes. So I could have seen 16 sunrises and sunsets each 24 hours I was in space.

Setting Sun. *Earth's atmosphere changes color as the sun sets.*

Sun Storm. *Bright arches of hot gas explode from the surface of the sun.*

Our Starry Neighbor

From Earth, the sun is the brightest object in the sky. It is also the largest object in our solar system. Yet the sun is just an average-size star. Stars are giant, glowing balls of hot gases. These gases are a star's fuel. Most stars' fuel lasts for billions of years.

Stars like our sun change these gases into energy. We see and feel this energy as heat and light. It takes a little more than eight minutes for the sun's light to reach Earth. That means the sunlight you are seeing now left the sun about eight minutes ago.

Spots on the Sun

The sun might look like it is calm and quiet. Think again! When we use a **telescope**, we can see the sun up close. Now the sun looks alive with activity. Gases boil and bubble. Fiery storms rage.

One kind of storm, called sunspots, looks like dark blotches. A sunspot looks dark because it's cooler than the areas around it. The number of spots follows an 11-year cycle. At times, many sunspots speckle the sun. At other times, we can't see any.

Our Solar System

Energy from the sun doesn't only warm Earth. It warms all the planets. A planet is a large space object that orbits a star. In all, eight planets orbit our sun. Four of these planets are small, rocky worlds. They're called the inner planets.

The other four are giant planets made of gases. They're called the outer planets. Jupiter is the largest of these worlds. It is almost completely made of gases. Its Great Red Spot is one of the largest storms on any planet in the solar system.

Star Light, Star Bright

From space, I had a good view of the planets, the sun, and many stars. From Earth, stars seem to twinkle. That's because gases in Earth's atmosphere are always moving.

In space, every star shines bright and steady. They also shine with different colors. A star's color tells how hot it is. Cooler stars are reddish. Warmer stars are yellow. Hotter stars are blue.

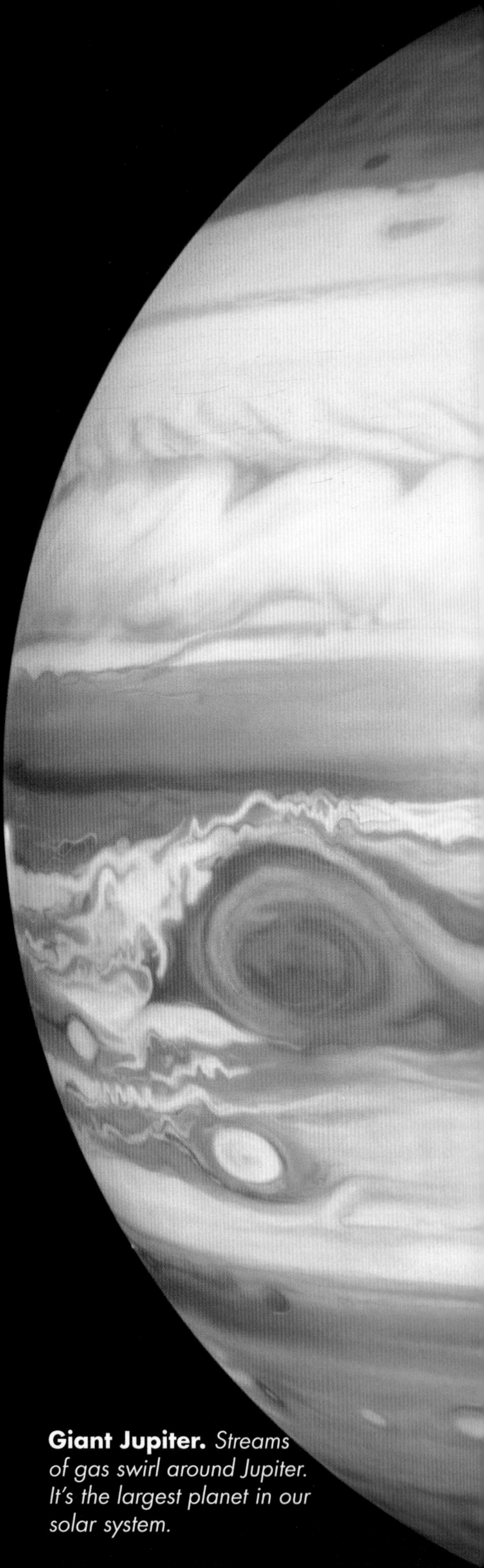

Giant Jupiter. *Streams of gas swirl around Jupiter. It's the largest planet in our solar system.*

A Star Is Born

Space is the best place to study stars. The Hubble Space Telescope orbits in space. It takes photos of stars. Some of Hubble's best photos show nebulae.

A nebula is a cloud of gas and dust in space. Stars form within some nebulae. It takes millions of years to make a star. It starts with **gravity**.

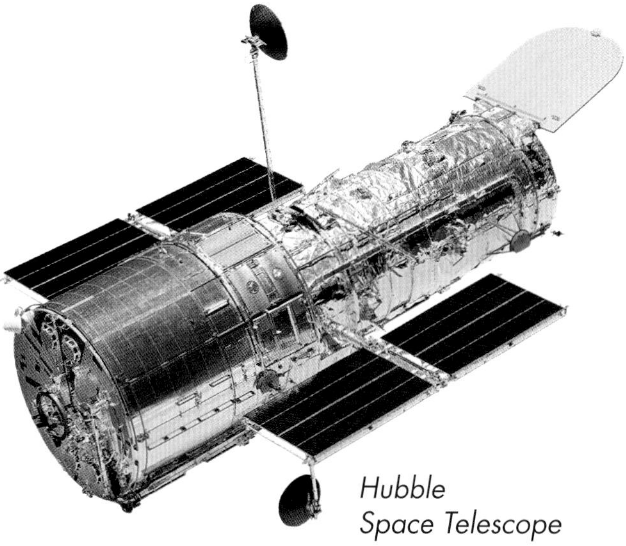

Hubble Space Telescope

Gravity is a pulling force. All objects have it. Inside the nebula, gravity pulls bits of gas and dust together. The pull of gravity gets stronger. The mass, or amount of stuff, attracts more space stuff.

The mass grows larger. Gravity pulls harder. It begins to press everything into a tight ball. The ball grows blazing hot. It starts to shine. A star is born.

Star Babies. *New stars are born in the Carina Nebula.*

Dying Stars

Most stars live for millions or billions of years. How long a star lives depends on how big it is. The largest and hottest stars have the shortest lives. Our sun is about halfway through its life. It will probably burn for five billion more years.

Galaxies Ahead

A group of millions of stars is called a **galaxy**. Our solar system is in the Milky Way galaxy.

Hubble has shown us some other amazing galaxies. Many look like spirals. One is shaped like a tadpole. Another looks like the eye of a cat.

Last Breath. *The Helix Nebula is a ring of gas around a dying star.*

Star Burst. *An exploding giant star formed the Crab Nebula.*

A star's size also affects how it dies. Eventually stars use up all their fuel. Smaller stars just fizzle. Some really big stars cave in on themselves. Scientists call these explosions supernovas.

The largest stars can create black holes. Black holes are small, dense objects. No one knows exactly what happens inside black holes. Their gravity is super strong. Not even light can escape them.

From the window of *Columbia*, the sky looked alive with stars. One night, I gazed at two small galaxies near the Milky Way. I had to look quickly. My view was about to change. Another sunrise was on its way.

I had seen many sights in space. Still, as amazing as stars, nebulae, and galaxies are, there's no place like home, our planet Earth.

Star Spiral. *Billions of stars make up the Whirlpool galaxy. Its arms are home to young stars. Older stars shine in its yellow center.*

WORDWISE

axis: line about which a rotating body such as Earth turns

galaxy: system of stars

gravity: pulling force that all objects have

rotation: act of turning around a center

telescope: device used to study distant objects

Powered by the Sun

BY ELIZABETH SENGEL

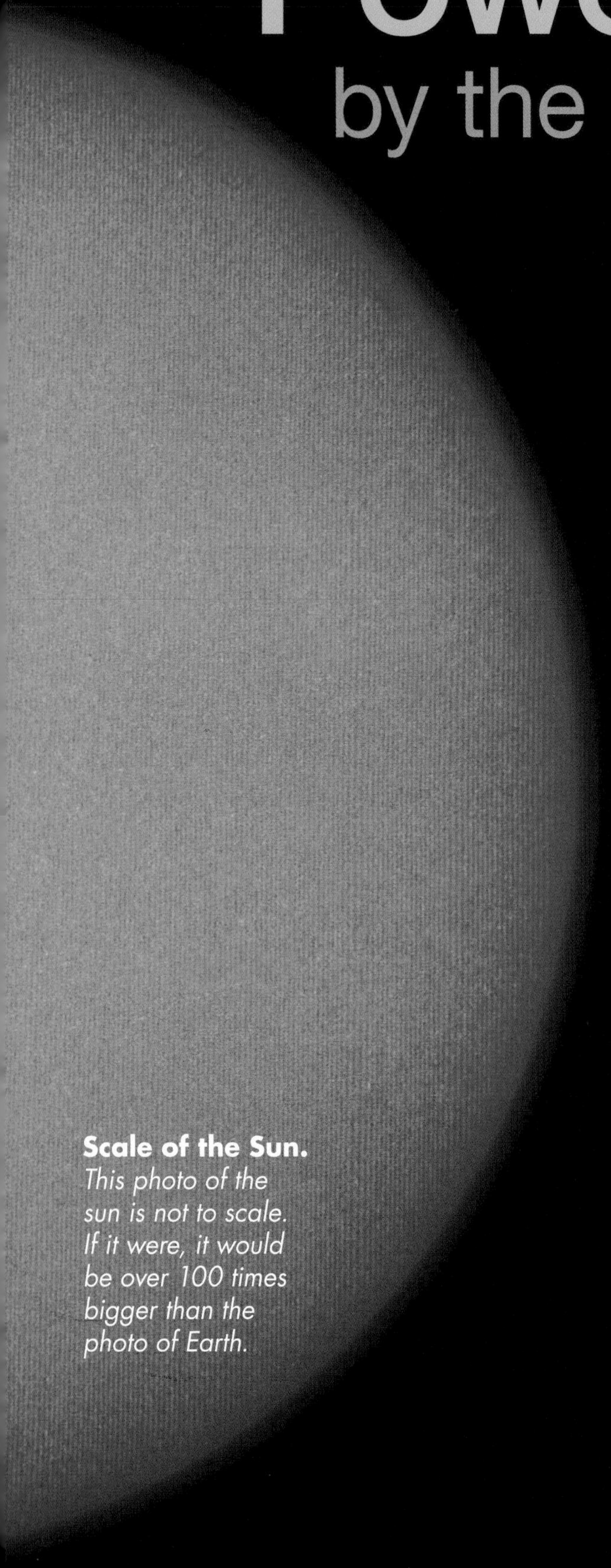

Scale of the Sun. *This photo of the sun is not to scale. If it were, it would be over 100 times bigger than the photo of Earth.*

The International Space Station (ISS) glides 386 kilometers (240 miles) above Earth. A crew lives and does research on the ISS. How does this amazing spacecraft get the electricity it needs to keep everything running?

The answer is the sun. The ISS has eight solar arrays, or panels. These huge structures look like wings. They are covered with 262,400 solar cells. A solar cell is a tiny device that changes sunlight into electricity.

Sometimes the ISS is in Earth's shadow. Then the crew members use batteries to get power. The batteries are recharged when the spacecraft moves back into the sunlight again.

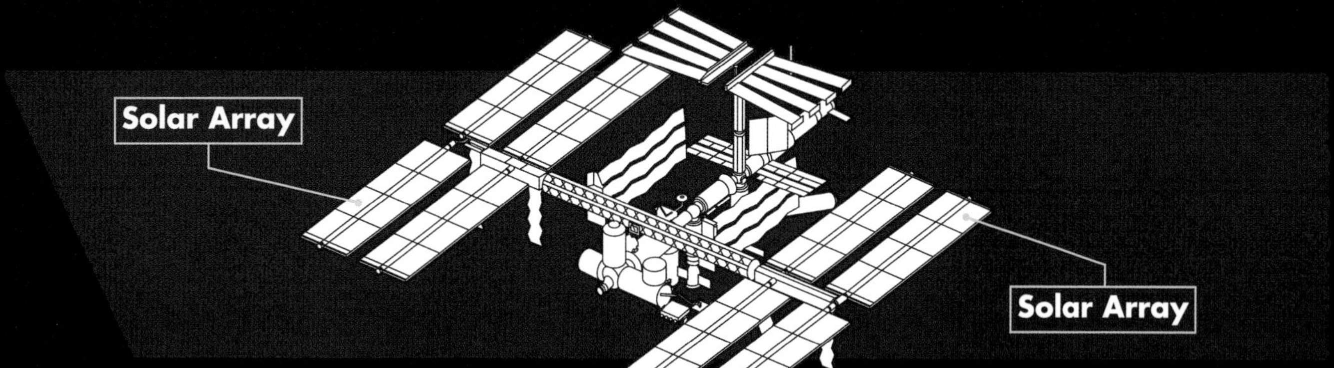

International Space Station

Look Closely. *This is what a solar array looks like up close.*

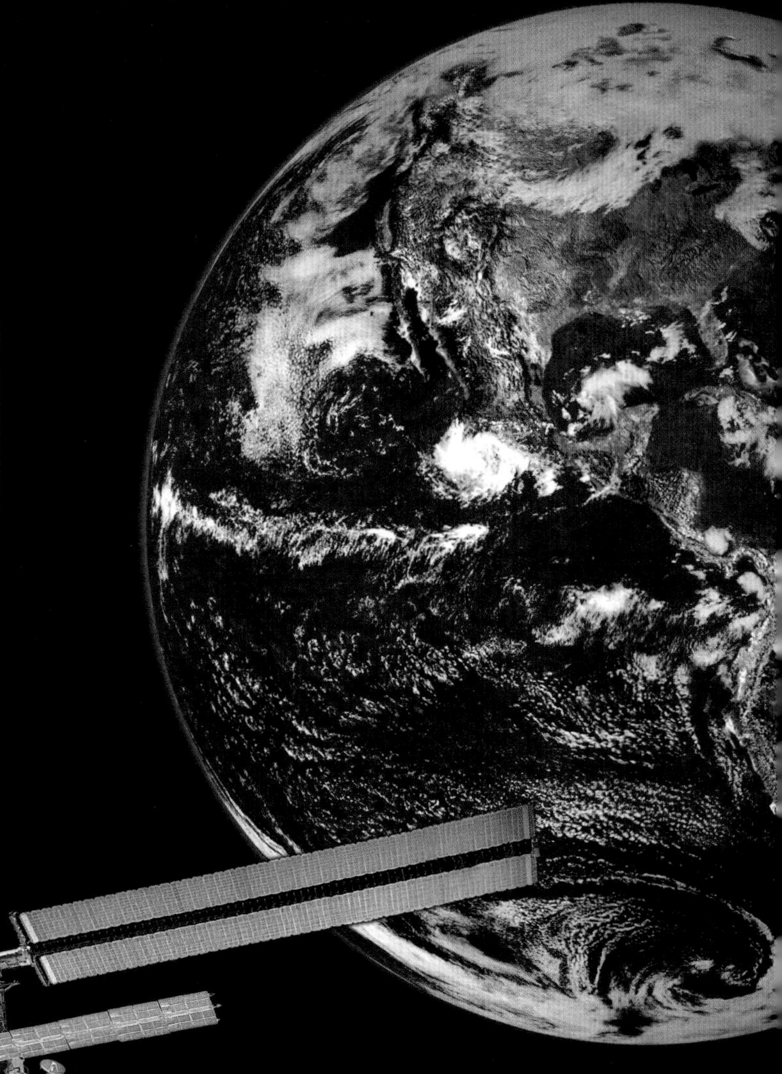
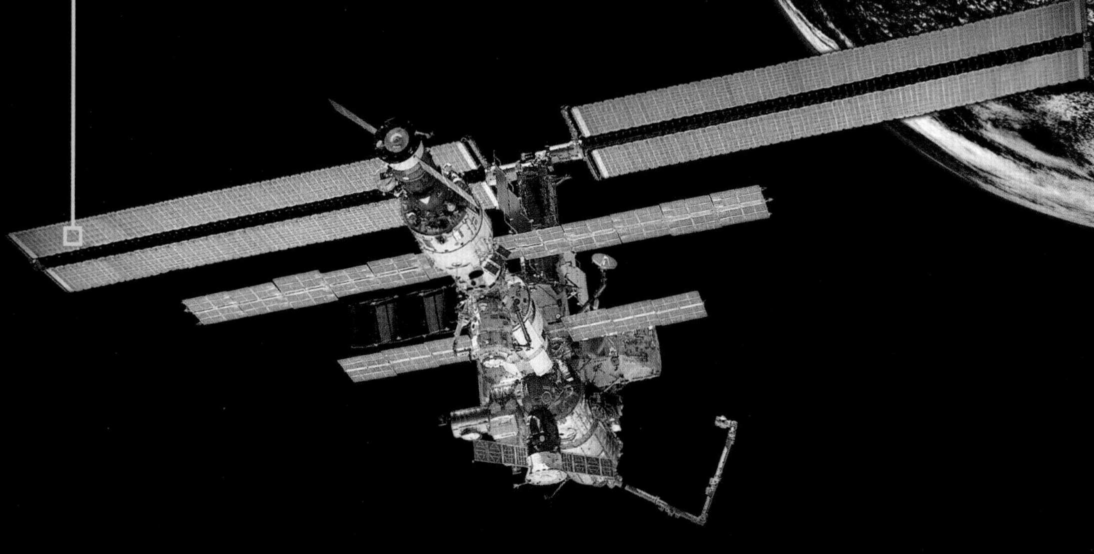

Shining STAR

Follow the stars. Then answer these questions about the sun and its energy.

1. What are stars made of? How do stars make energy?
2. How do stars form?
3. Stars die in different ways. Name two ways that a star's size can affect how it dies.
4. Why does Don Thomas say there is no place like Earth?
5. What are solar arrays? What do they look like?